My Grandma and Me

MINA JAVAHERBIN

illustrated by
LINDSEY YANKEY

CANDLEWICK PRESS

When I was growing up in Iran, my grandma lived with us. I followed her everywhere. When she swept, I swept. When she cooked, I cooked. When she prayed, I prayed like her, too.

At dawn, when she woke up for namaz, I woke up with her, too.
"Praying at dawn is my favorite," she would say with a smile.
"Mine too!" I would say with a wider smile.

Because only the two of us were up at that time, and no one was there to stop me, I would climb up and lie on her back while she prayed.

My grandma never told me to stop or broke out of her prayers. Instead, she sat up gently each time, making sure that I didn't fall.

After her namaz, we kept watch for the bread delivery boy. He piled the bread high on his bike like a clever acrobatic act.

But my grandma and I had a clever act, too. We bought fresh bread every day without leaving our third-floor apartment!

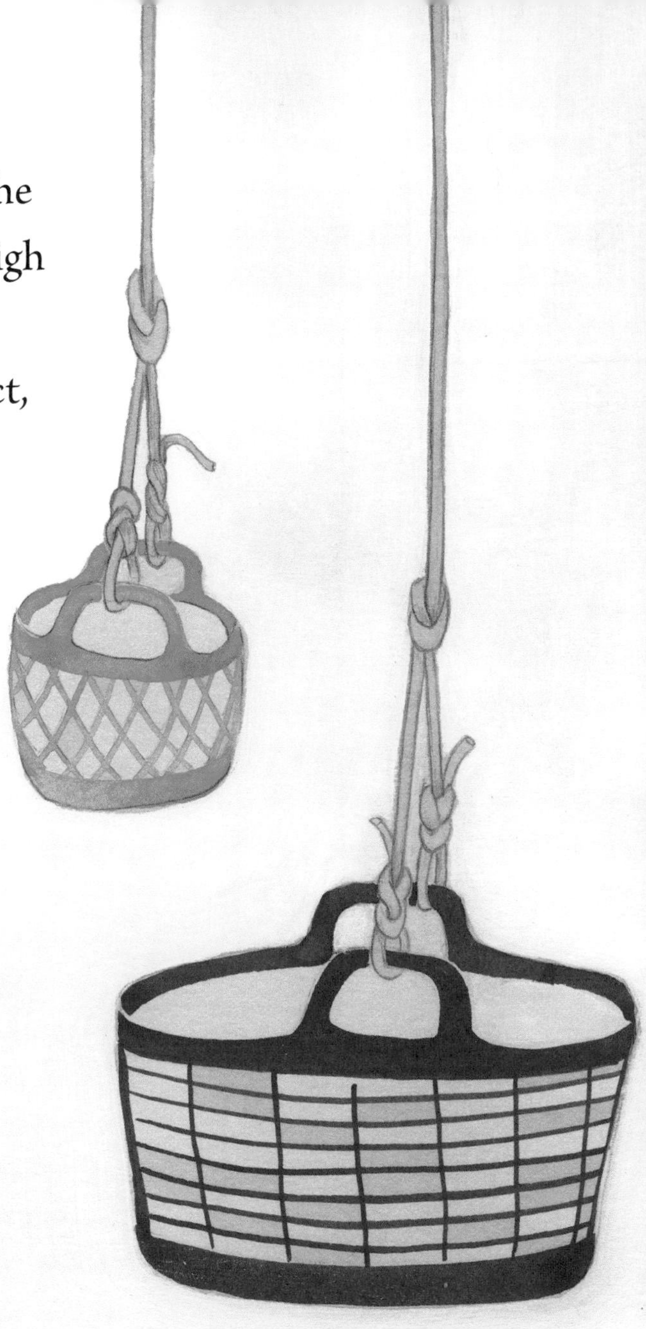

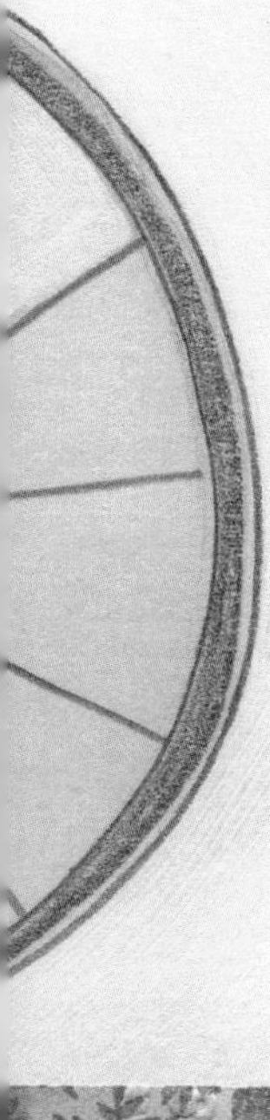

We sent our baskets down with ropes, the bread boy placed the bread inside, and then we hauled them up.

My grandma's basket was so big, I could fit inside it. I would sit in that basket and pretend to be flying my own plane.

My doll played, too.

Once the bread arrived, my doll, my grandma, and I would take some to my friend Annette, next door.

Like Annette and me, our grandmas were best friends. They enjoyed each other's company. Every day while we played together, they talked, laughed, and drank coffee.

Our grandmas knitted blankets together
as they watched us play hopscotch in the alley.
They donated them to my grandma's mosque
and Annette's grandma's church.

From the end of the alley, we could see their heads bent over the blankets — Annette's grandma with her silver hair and my grandma in her favorite chador, the white one with small purple flowers.

My grandma had all kinds of chadors. She wore them for different occasions. For parties and mosque, she wore a black one, made of fancy crepe fabric. It was heavy, soft, and cool to the touch. It looked like a magical cape. My grandma sewed all her own chadors.

And I helped.

Mostly I helped by draping her chadors on the table to build my rocket ship.

Or tying her chador around my neck so I could fly from the moon to planets. I was a super-astro-explorer! My grandma was always waiting for me back at the base camp with cookies. We ate together while I told her about my space adventures.

During the holy month of Ramadan, my grandma did not eat from dawn to dusk. When she woke up to eat, before sunrise, I woke up to eat, too.

"You're too young to fast just yet," she said to me. I ate with my grandma anyway. Then I ate as usual during the day, and after dusk, at iftar time, I ate with her again!

One time, when I was a little older and finally fasted with her, in the middle of the dark and somber night, I wore the chador she made me and we walked together to the mosque.

Inside, the lights shone bright, and no one was quiet or somber. People laughed and ate and talked until it was time for prayers. My grandma prayed for Annette's grandma. She prayed that Annette's grandma would go to heaven.

After the prayers, there was tea and milk and dates and sherbet and cookies. In the mosque's kitchen, volunteers cooked rice and stew in giant copper pots. Some ate at the mosque, while others took the food home. We filled a dish, and on the way home, my grandma left it for a man sleeping on the sidewalk. As we walked away, she said a prayer for the sick and poor in the world.

The next morning when I saw Annette, she whispered a secret to me: "Last night at the church, my grandma prayed for your grandma to go to heaven!"

My eyes widened. "My grandma did the same thing at the mosque!"

Annette and I looked up. Our grandmas were talking and drinking coffee together. I could imagine them knitting and laughing together anywhere — on Earth, on Mars, or in heaven.

In this big universe full of many moons, I have traveled and seen many wonders, but I've never loved anything or anyone the way I loved my grandma. She was kind, generous, and full of love. I still want to be just like her.

To my beloved grandma Batool
M. J.

To Ashton
L. Y.

Author's Note

As in most cultures, Iranians use various terms or endearing names for their grandmothers. The most usual one is *maman-bozorg,* which just means "grandma." My grandpa used to call my grandma *Khanom,* which means "lady," to show his respect for her, and so my father and uncle grew up calling her that as well. And when I came along, I called her *Khanom,* too. To me, my grandma was indeed a lady — noble, dignified, graceful, and kind.

Illustrator's Note

I have been blessed with two grandmas in this life, and illustrating Mina's story has stirred up my own fond memories. I will always remember my grandma Brooks's hoot of laughter and her kindness. And with each visit, I admire the twinkle in my grandma Jeanne's eyes when my son blows her a kiss.

First US paperback edition 2022

Library of Congress Catalog Card Number 2018962890
ISBN 978-0-7636-9494-4 (hardcover)
ISBN 978-1-5362-2355-2 (paperback)

APS 27 26 25 24 23 22
10 9 8 7 6 5 4 3 2 1

Printed in Humen, Dongguan, China

This book was typeset in Brioso Medium.
The illustrations were done in mixed media.

Candlewick Press
99 Dover Street
Somerville, Massachusetts 02144

visit us at www.candlewick.com